A MINDFUL LIFE

A MINDFUL LIFE

WHO'S THIS IN THE SHOWER WITH ME? HOW TO GET
OUT OF YOUR HEAD AND START LIVING

The Happy Buddha

© 2017 by The Happy Buddha
All rights reserved.

ISBN: 1974326950
ISBN 13: 9781974326952
Library of Congress Control Number: 2017912355
CreateSpace Independent Publishing Platform
North Charleston, South Carolina

ABOUT THE AUTHOR

The Happy Buddha (Suryacitta) was born Malcolm Smith in northern England in 1960. After working in market stalls, selling records and CDs, he came across meditation in a local library. He started practicing mindfulness in 1989, and ten years later, he was ordained into the Triratna Buddhist Order on a four-month retreat in Spain and given the name Suryacitta. In 2000, he decided to dedicate the next years to meditation, and he lived and taught in a secluded meditation retreat center in north Wales, in the United Kingdom, where he wrote his first book.

He left the retreat center in 2005 and moved to Brighton in southern England. There he met Gaynor, whom he later married. Gaynor and Suryacitta decided to move to Leicestershire to be near her family. Here he wrote his second book.

They spend their time running their not-for-profit business and walking their lovely dog, Jaya.

Suryacitta and Gaynor now teach in the United Kingdom, Europe, and Australia.

Suryacitta is the author of two books, *Happiness and How It Happens—Finding Contentment Through Mindfulness* (2011) and *Mindfulness and Compassion—Embracing Life with Loving Kindness* (2015), both published by Ivy Press.

See his website: www.mindfulnesscic.co.uk.

Contact: Suryacitta@gmail.com.

I would like to dedicate this book to Charlotte Joko Beck for her simple, elegant, and beautiful teachings.

CONTENTS

About The Author······································v
About This Book···································xiii

MINDFULNESS MEDITATION ················ 1
What's Wrong with Right Now? ················ 3
The Forgotten Medicine ······················ 6
Grandmother Mind······························ 8
Unminding··································13
The Vending Machine·························15
Horse Manure·······························17
Mindfulness and Concentration ···············19
Fiddling and Standing Back ················ 22
Living Matters·····························24
Mirror in the Bathroom ···················· 26
Creating a Container························ 28

THOUGHTS ································ 33
I Can't Stand This Anymore ················ 35
Dirty Cars ································ 38
Happy Birthday····························· 40

The Mind Is like a Hammer · · · · · · · · · · · · · · · · · 42
The Heady Professor · 45
Taking Down the Scaffolding of Thought · · · · · · · · ·47
Help, I Can't Stop Thinking! · · · · · · · · · · · · · · · · 50
Help, I Can't Sleep Either! · · · · · · · · · · · · · · · · · 54

FEELINGS ·57
Pushing Our Buttons ·59
Anxiety—Is It True or False? · · · · · · · · · · · · · · · 62
Melting the Ice · 65
Not Running Away Anymore · · · · · · · · · · · · · · · 69
Upadana — Do I Do That? · · · · · · · · · · · · · · · · ·71
Dog Shit, Transformation, and the Plum Tree · · · · · ·74
Your Real Home ·78
The Search and What's Driving It · · · · · · · · · · · · ·81

A MINDFUL LIFE · 83
Texting or Nexting · 85
Who's This in the Shower with Me? · · · · · · · · · · · 88
Looking for the Key · 92
Is That So? · 95
Retro Mindfulness—The Forgotten Art of Pausing · · 97
The Meditation Master and the Vase · · · · · · · · · · 101
A Crack in It ·104
The Difference between Heaven and Hell · · · · · · · ·108
The Roots of Mindfulness · · · · · · · · · · · · · · · · 110
The Four Truths of Life · · · · · · · · · · · · · · · · · · 111
Does a Dog Have Mindfulness? · · · · · · · · · · · · ·116

Mindful Walking and the Bird Feeder · · · · · · · · · · · 118
The Lazy Fisherman · 120
Riders on the Storm · 121
How to Be Totally Unhappy Right Now and Forever · · 125
How to Be (a Little) Happier Right Now and Forever · · 127
Giving · 129
Kisa Gotami and the Mustard Seed · · · · · · · · · · · 132

Thanks · 135
A Mindful Life...Join The Community · · · · · · · · · · 137

ABOUT THIS BOOK

WE HAVE THIS life. We may have others or not; I don't know, and really, I don't think about it that much. What I do know is that I am here living this life now. The problem is that most of us are not here while it is happening. Our minds are restless. Our attention is hijacked again and again by our restless mind. We live what I call an unmindful life, a life where distraction is the norm, which leads us to feeling dissatisfied and unfulfilled, as if something is missing.

This book and the events I run are aimed at changing this. They are aimed at learning to live a mindful life—a life where we are present while we are living it. This book has been written to help each of us replace agitation with contentment, to replace restlessness and worry with ease and joy.

Mindfulness, for me, is beautiful; it is like a jewel. Each story in this book emphasizes a particular facet of the jewel of mindfulness; one story does not give the whole picture. As we read and as we practice our meditation, we discover new facets of the jewel. But the point is that we never stop discovering; the living of a mindful life is a long and rich journey.

The stories and teachings in this book are from my own life, the lives of others, and my own observations about the joys and sorrows of this life.

The stories and anecdotes in this book follow four themes: mindfulness meditation, thoughts, feelings, and a mindful life. But each story and teaching stands alone too. So feel free to read from beginning to end or just dip into it at leisure. I suggest, though, that you read them slowly. Allow yourself to be moved and to feel them as you read. In other words, read them with your heart, not your head.

This book of course can be read alone. But it is also an entry point to a program I have developed, called A Mindful Life. The program can be accessed from anywhere in the world and includes live online meditation and discussion evenings, access to all webinars I run, and online courses. You can find out more at the end of the book.

The stories and anecdotes are punctuated with short meditations.

Please do them as you go through the book.

MINDFULNESS MEDITATION

WHAT'S WRONG WITH RIGHT NOW?

MEDITATION IS VERY misunderstood. Most human beings spend most of their time exploring and thinking about some other time, some other life, in some other place. We spend more time thinking and dreaming about the life we don't have than living the one we do.

Meditation turns this around. It is learning to pay attention to what is going on here and now. Often, we are walking down the street, having a shower, dressing the kids, or washing our body, but we are doing something else with the mind. We may be drinking a cup of coffee and arguing with the boss at the same time.

We may be vacuuming the stairs and dreaming of our holiday simultaneously. We are rarely here doing the activity with both our body and mind.

A friend of mine runs yoga retreats in the Caribbean. The venue is in a beautiful location on a purpose-made hotel terrace overlooking the ocean. When he gets clients there, he tells them that they have probably been thinking about this place for a few months, looking forward to it. They have been in their day jobs and dreaming of being here on the beach and doing yoga—wonderful! During the sessions of yoga, however, he asks them where their attention is now, and most of them admit to him that it is not here. It is somewhere else. They are at their dream place, but they are not here. They are now thinking of something or somewhere else—eating dinner, going home, thinking about their job, checking for texts, and so on.

This is the human condition. We do not like to be here with how life is. We prefer to create this abstract life in our head so that we can think about life rather than feel and experience it. When we take up meditation, the instruction is to notice when our attention wanders away from the moment to thinking about something. Then we return the attention back to the object of attention—the breath, sounds, and sensations in the body. It doesn't matter much what the object is; what is important is that we are learning to be in the here and now, learning to pay attention.

We sit in meditation and then *bing*. We are away in some fantasy or worry. We label those thoughts as thinking and then return (we will go into that further in the rest of the book). We turn back to now, to this, to what is happening. We don't like it because it is not exciting. Being with the breath is not going to be that entertaining to us. We prefer the drama of our own mind. We are not fussy whether the drama is excitement about a holiday or worries and anxieties about something going on—or not going on—in our life. We are just addicted to thinking, to the drama; it makes us feel alive. But it is unsatisfactory. It doesn't bring us peace and contentment. We cannot live our life in fantasy. It is not real. Only real life, being here and now with the unpleasant and the pleasant, can bring us real satisfaction. Meditation, then, is not complicated; it is the simplest thing there is but tricky for our restless and clever minds.

Practice this: Feel the breath as it is, or listen to a sound. It doesn't really matter what we pay attention to. Now have a look at what is so wrong or bad or difficult about the right now until you start thinking about it. Don't take my word for it; try it. What is so wrong with right now unless you think about something "better" or about how bad and boring it is?

What we come to see is that our views, opinions, and judgments about this moment make it difficult. If we take away our judgments or at least observe them rather than indulging them each moment, it is much more bearable and over time more enjoyable.

THE FORGOTTEN MEDICINE

According to mental-health organizations, there are more and more of us experiencing some level of mental fatigue and even illness. Even younger people are now suffering from stress and anxieties.

I am sure that there are many good ways of dealing with this. Many therapies, counseling, and even pills may help in some cases.

However, another medicine is little known, but it has been around for a few thousand years. That medicine is what we call "mindfulness." I am certainly not advocating that it replace conventional ways of treating our troubles, but it is an excellent medicine—one we have forgotten about.

Most of us spend our days rushing from one thing to another, never resting. Often our view is that we are doing very important things, and of course, some things are and do need doing. But I wonder what is driving this activity, necessity, or the inability to sit still—in other words, restlessness.

If our lives are full of activity, then our heads will be full of thoughts. Living in this way leaves us often feeling agitated, tired, and even ill.

The medicine of mindfulness encourages us to sit still or at least to take pauses during the day. Sitting still and not trying to achieve anything a few times a day allows our minds to rest and our emotions to heal.

The medicine of mindfulness can be taken in the workplace, at home, on the bus, or waiting in a queue.

So each day, sit down, stop rushing around, and do what the Buddha, the great physician of the mind, ordered and take the medicine of silence and stillness.

GRANDMOTHER MIND

Sobo Maindo is a Japanese term meaning "grandmother mind," and according to the mindfulness tradition, it is something we all need to develop. Our own happiness is dependent on developing *Sobo Maindo*.

When I was a young boy, my mum used to take me to see my grandmother. She was always "gran" to me. My mum would open the door, I would run in, and my gran would say, "Come here, son," and give me a big kiss. She would open her arms and give me a big cuddle. I used to love going to my gran's home. She may have been the same with all her grandchildren, but I didn't care. I knew she loved me.

My mum would sometimes say, "He has been naughty, you know. He hasn't washed behind his ears, or he didn't brush his teeth last night." But it didn't matter to my grandmother.

She would say, "I don't care. Come here, son, and give me a kiss." She would say to my mum, "You go and do your shopping and leave him with me."

Sobo Maindo as you may have guessed translates as "grandmother mind." This is what we all need to develop. Just as my gran welcomed everything about me, so we need to do the same with ourselves. It is not that she would never say to me to go wash, darling, or that she never corrected me when I was naughty. But that she loved me anyway.

In our mindfulness practice, we need this same attitude. It may be self-criticism, or it may be tears, failure, embarrassment, shame, sadness, or joy. But what we need is to meet our experience with grandmother mind.

Grandmother mind is the mind of compassion. It doesn't judge, it doesn't condemn or criticize, and it doesn't pick faults or gossip about people. Grandmother mind is open and warm; it welcomes everything into its embrace. Grandmother mind is discerning but not judgmental.

Often, we turn away from our own difficult emotions. The last thing we want to do is to open our hearts to something we don't like; however, this is the very thing we need to do if we are to stop the inner conflict that we find ourselves in.

When we are experiencing difficult emotions, most of us have a tendency to stay in our heads. We try to work it all out and we try to scheme, but the grandmother mind lives in the heart. However, if we stay in the head with its stories, opinions, and judgments, we cannot hear the heart and hear what it is saying.

The heart always welcomes whatever is happening, no matter how much it hurts. As well as being the place of gentleness and welcoming, the heart is also the place of courage. If we talk about people who have shown courage in life, we never say they have a brave head but instead a brave heart.

If we can learn to live in the heart, then we learn to live not only more compassionately but also more courageously.

Our compassion meditation again and again takes us from the abstract world of our head to the real world of the heart and the land of feeling.

Practice this: Find a quiet place where you won't be disturbed. Sit still and comfortably. You can put a timer on if that helps for around ten minutes.

Just have a sense of yourself sitting here. This is you in this moment. The whole of your life has brought you to this point right here and now.

Take your attention to your heart area, the center of your chest. Sense this area, and see how it feels. Just keep sensing this area. How does it feel? Tight, tense, open, relaxed, warm, sad, nothing? No matter what is there, welcome it, even if you are unsure about what is there. Welcome that sense of being unsure; do your best not to turn away. Do this for around five minutes. You can include the breath here too.

Now gradually shift your attention, and look for something in your experience that is a little uncomfortable. Just a little, nothing too big. It may be a tight hip, an aching knee, or a tightness somewhere. Or it may be something in your heart area that you have just discovered. If nothing is there, perhaps bring to mind something in your life that has troubled you a little recently. Maybe you said something a little unkind, or you were a little selfish at some point. Notice how it makes you feel in the body, and allow yourself to feel it.

Let it be there for a minute or two. Then shift your attention, and look for something pleasant. There will be something, even if it is the lips resting gently together or the breath. Perhaps the quietness is pleasant.

Now allow the pleasant and the unpleasant to be there. We can be courageous enough to sit with both the pleasant and the unpleasant. This is a metaphor for our life. We have unpleasantness and the pleasantness.

We can hold both of them without pushing away the unpleasant and wanting more of the pleasant.

In this way, we develop our grandmother mind. Not that ordinarily we go looking for unpleasantness, but when it is here, we can respond to it rather than react out of habit.

UNMINDING

We can see meditation as a process of what I call "unminding." All day long, we are what we could call "minding." We are in the mind thinking about this, that, and the other. All this thinking leaves us confused and can leave us exhausted.

Not all thinking, of course, does this; there is useful thinking, creative thinking, and reflective thinking. But most of our thinking is actually unconscious drivel that passes through the mind, commenting on almost everything we do and everything we see. The judging mind is so powerful. We see somebody, and immediately there is a judgment. People often try not to judge, but that is not good practice. The mind does judge, but we can just observe that happening.

However, I digress. When we are in the mind, minding, it can create a lot of stress and agitation. So we each need periods of what I call unminding. Unminding is where we simply rest our attention on one of the senses.

Let us say sounds or the feeling of the breeze on the skin. Or of course, it can be the breath.

This unminding allows unwinding to take place and gives us the opportunity to see what is going on in our life.

THE VENDING MACHINE

MOST OF US treat our meditation as if it were a vending machine. With a vending machine, you put your money in, and then you get a can of cola or orange instantly. We can use a vending machine every day and get what we want. It is a straightforward exchange. Occasionally, though, you will put your money in, and nothing happens. So you kick, slap, and even curse it—it is so unfair!

Most of us approach meditation and indeed our life in a similar way that we approach a vending machine. We do our meditation and put something into life, and we want something back. And to a degree, this is understandable and sometimes works. However, the more we try to engineer our meditation to match our ideas of how it should be, the more disappointed we become.

Meditation is not meant to give us everything we want. You cannot always have the weather you want, the food you want, the person you want. We cannot always feel how we want.

If you approach your practice as you approach a vending machine, then I am afraid you won't get very far.

So how should we approach it? Well, we do the practice, and that is it. The best way to practice is simply to do it and be aware of the desire to achieve something. Meditation reveals our hidden agenda of wanting to get something. These hidden agendas run our lives. So instead of meditation being another activity to fulfill our neurotic needs, we become aware of them and don't feed them.

Why not try this *let-me-see* approach rather than the vending-machine approach and see what happens?

HORSE MANURE

I was once running a retreat in the south of England at a large garden center with beautiful flowers, shrubs, and trees from around the world. In many ways, it was an ideal location, with both silence and beauty.

While sitting quietly in the garden one day, I noticed in the yard a large pile of horse manure. It looked almost like a pyramid from a distance.

The manure was not very useful sitting where it was in the yard. At some point, of course, they would begin to sprinkle it around the gardens, placing it around the roots of the plants.

This got me thinking that mindfulness is similar to horse manure. Once the manure has been spread around, then everything in the garden benefits from the manure. All the plants become stronger, brighter, and more robust.

Likewise, when we practice mindfulness, everything in our life begins to benefit. Not immediately, but gradually over time, just like the plants.

What I mean is that when we practice mindfulness, we are working on our mind; we are nourishing it.

Now, you might think, "So how does that benefit the whole of our life?" Well, the quality of the soil determines the quality of the plants. Healthy soil, healthy plants. It is the same with our mind. If we have a healthy mind, we have a healthier life. I don't mean a perfect life I just mean one that is healthier.

We don't do anything without the mind; everything we do, we do it with the mind. Whether it is running, gardening, painting, teaching, or talking. Whatever, we take our mind with us everywhere we go.

So if we nourish the mind through daily practice of mindfulness, the whole of our life benefits. We become a little stronger, a little wiser, and a little kinder to others and ourselves. We become more present, a little more patient, and a little more courageous.

So this is why mindfulness is like horse manure.

MINDFULNESS AND CONCENTRATION

I was leading a retreat in Scotland in 2012, and a woman came in for a meditation interview and said she was a little upset because people were making noise when leaving the shrine room and it was disturbing her meditation. I responded of course and asked people to leave as quietly as possible in consideration for other people. The woman had some experience of meditation, so in the meditation review, I talked to her about the difference between mindfulness and concentration.

My point to the woman mentioned above is that we need to think in terms of both concentration and mindfulness when we sit to meditate. My view was that she was overly concerned with concentration at the expense of mindfulness. This can make meditation quite brittle.

If I am leaning toward concentration and not taking mindfulness into account, then I can get upset or think that my meditation has been disturbed. Concentration can obviously be disturbed as it is by nature a steadiness of mind on an object. It seems to me that if my concentration takes place within the context of mindfulness, then that disturbance is merely noted as another event arising. The way I see it is that mindfulness cannot be disturbed, but my focus or concentration can be. This does not mean that concentration, in my view, is unnecessary but needs to be held with mindfulness.

This approach has helped me be less precious about my meditation around outside influences. I remember trying to explain this when running a retreat at Vajraloka retreat center. The meditation afterward was so very quiet, as it often was, and I sat there kind of hoping that a pheasant would come close to the meditation room and start its shrieking or a tractor would come chugging by just to illustrate the difference between mindfulness and concentration. I was trying to describe that a noise may arise (as they do in everyday life) and the mind will react, but the movement of mind can be noted and so too can the emotional reaction. If I am attached to concentration and something happens around me, then that can give rise to a negative emotional reaction if I deem my concentration has been disturbed.

It seems to me that in some way concentration is the activity of mindfulness, but without mindfulness, it can lack wisdom and compassion or intelligence and kindness, and perhaps mindfulness without the ability to concentrate can lack a kind of focus or purpose or everyday functioning. We can concentrate without mindfulness, but if we are mindful, then we have the ability to concentrate. Another way of seeing it is that mindfulness is the container in which concentration can happen, but without the container, then it's all pretty chaotic.

What I was trying to explain to the woman on retreat was that within those very few moments of disturbance, we can see the four noble truths.

1. There is suffering (a little in this case).
2. There is a cause of suffering—her not wanting the sound to be happening.
3. There is end of suffering—if she dropped her resistance to what was going on.
4. How to the end suffering—attending to her situation (in the meditation room) with mindfulness.

There is more about these truths later on.

FIDDLING AND STANDING BACK

I AM SURE most of us are familiar with flower arranging. If you have not arranged a vase of flowers yourself, you will at least have seen it done. My wife, Gaynor, often arranges flowers for the retreats we lead.

One particular morning, I was sitting preparing for a retreat and sipping my cup of Yorkshire tea. I was watching Gaynor arrange the flowers. She would fiddle with them and stand back. She would fiddle a little more and stand back again. She did this four or five times, and then when she was happy with them, she would put them onto the shrine in the meditation space.

Now, she had to fiddle with the flowers or else they would not have looked pretty. But what was the point of her standing back? Well, she had to stand back to see how they looked in relation to each other, the vase, and the room.

The fiddling is absolutely essential, but so is the standing back. The standing back and just looking gave her a perspective on the flowers that she would not get if she had just been up close and fiddling with them.

When watching her, I thought what she was doing was a good way of explaining meditation. In life, we have to fiddle; in other words, we have to be active—we have to be in the doing mode some of the time or else nothing would get done. But there are times when we need to just stand back from life. This is what meditation is about. When we sit in meditation or, indeed, when we come back to awareness in daily life, we are in a way standing back from life. We observe ourselves instead of just being lost in doing. So when we sit in meditation for twenty minutes, we get a chance to see our life from a different perspective—one of being and observing instead of doing. But when we meditate, we are also standing back from something else; we are "standing back" from our own experience. We are observing our own thoughts and emotions instead of being lost in them.

LIVING MATTERS

It is very easy to think that a session of sitting meditation is separate from the rest of our life. That it is an isolated few minutes where we block out the rest of life. To some degree that is correct, as we take ourselves away from the usual disturbances, but in another way, it is very much connected to the rest of our life. When we sit in meditation, what we experience is how we have lived. We experience the effects of the minutes before, the hours before, and the weeks and the years prior to each session of meditation.

Our experience when we sit on the cushion is the result of the rest of our life. But it also affects the rest of our life. If we run around like mad things, then we will experience the results of that when we sit on the cushion.

If you act unkindly and unethically and you are being a pain to other people, then that is what you will get on the cushion. If you spend your time moaning, complaining, and gossiping about people, then that will affect your state of mind.

That is why in the Buddhist tradition we have guidelines for living; things such as speaking truthfully and kindly, not gossiping and being nasty to people.

What we practice during our daily life is what we will get on the cushion.

MIRROR IN THE BATHROOM

When you get up in the morning, you go to the bathroom. On your wall is probably a mirror. A mirror reflects back what is happening on the outside; you can see if you need a shave, if you need makeup, or if you need to get a haircut. Sometimes though, you may not want to look in the mirror. It can be a little weird if you look at your reflection too long. Who on earth is that? Well, mindfulness meditation is a mirror. Just like the mirror on your wall reflects back what is happening on the outside, so the mirror of meditation reflects back what is happening on the inside, and again, we don't always want to look.

Meditation does change us in a way that is quite mysterious, but it also reveals to us what is going on within. In fact, everything can be a mirror. Sometimes I meditate by just staring at a white wall. From the usual point of view, this would be classed as madness—take him away before he loses it completely! But that wall becomes a mirror for me to see what is happening in my mind. If I have opinions and judgments about the wall, they are my opinions and judgments.

Other people can be a mirror if we know how to look. If they push our buttons, what does that say about us? If we criticize and slander other people, it says more about us than it does about them. After all, we have thought it and said it. I am not suggesting here that we should never come back to people if they have genuinely wronged us, just the opposite. If we don't, that says something; if we don't stand up for ourselves, then that says something about us too.

Remember, everything that we say and do says something about ourselves and not the other person. This is taking responsibility for our life and happiness.

Learn to observe yourself without judging yourself, and you will learn a great deal about who and how you are.

CREATING A CONTAINER

WHAT IS IT we are really trying to do when we take up meditation? It really doesn't matter which practice we do; we are always engaged in one thing: developing awareness, or put another way, we are cultivating the capacity to observe ourselves as we go through our life. What are we observing? Our mind, our speech, and our actions.

The most useful way I have come across to look at this comes from Zen teacher Charlotte Joko Beck. She says we are building a container for our life.

If we look at a human being, there are in fact a number of containers. We could say the mind is a container for our thoughts; our body is a container for the emotions and the rest of our psychological stuff.

However, another container is often overlooked because it is not a thing. We can call it mindfulness or awareness. Awareness is actually a container for the whole of our life. Within awareness, our life is played out.

Awareness is a tricky thing to grasp. It is not a thing. It doesn't have a shape; it is the absence of shape. It doesn't have form; it is the absence of form. It has no color, sound, or smell. But nobody can deny the existence of awareness.

To talk about our practice as developing awareness is OK, but it is not *quite* accurate. Awareness is already here. You are already aware. When people take up the practice of mindfulness, they often *try* to be mindful, *try* to be aware. Again, this is not quite right and leads eventually to bad practice. Do this now—try not to be aware for thirty seconds. Impossible, isn't it? So we are not really trying to develop awareness. It is OK to talk in these terms, but if you are a teacher of mindfulness or a serious practitioner, then you need to know this or else you will confuse yourself and your students, and your practice will be limited. We use awareness, which is already present, to turn toward our own experience, to pay attention to the world around us. It is more about a willingness to engage in bringing awareness to our experience.

As our willingness to meet ourselves over and over again increases, we realize that something is changing. We find ourselves more at ease with the world around us and ourselves. Our practice transforms us, but not the way we think. If you think the path of meditation is easy, you have no idea what it involves. It turns your life upside down and inside out.

Most of us come along to practice with the view that we are going to get rid of all our unpleasant thoughts and feelings or going to change them into pleasant ones. That does happen to some degree. A lot of healing goes on as we practice. But the deeper transformation is about identification.

We all believe that we are our thoughts, our feelings, and our psychological stuff. That is who I am, we believe. Even if we are told we are not, we realize that we can watch our thoughts come and go. We still believe they are who we are. We are deeply attached.

In other words, if awareness is the container, we believe we are the contents within that container. Because at least we can experience the contents, we can see the thoughts, feel the feelings, and everything else that happens to us. There isn't anything else, is there?

Well, if there weren't awareness, how would you know any of these things? How would you know thoughts, experience feelings, and so on?

Awareness is like space. Space exists, but it is not a thing. If it did not exist, then nothing could exist. Everything needs space to exist within. When you walk into a room, what do you notice? The people, walls, carpet, tables, chairs, and so on. You don't really notice the space itself.

The way we view and experience ourselves is similar. We see only the contents, and if the contents are not very nice or always changing, unreliable, like they are, then it is not surprising that we find ourselves on rather wobbly ground.

Our practice, as we have seen, is not to change the contents—but they do change naturally as we practice—but to realize that they are in constant flux. As we see this time and again, we begin to intuitively sense something else—that we are the awareness too, which is the *knowing* of our experience. We have our experience, and we know we have an experience. Awareness is that knowing of it, but it is totally and completely overlooked.

As this process deepens, our attachment to the contents diminishes, and consequently, we experience a sense of ease because we are no longer defined by our thoughts, feelings, and all that makes up the contents.

So our practice is to see that we are not merely the contents. We welcome and treat the contents with kindness, but this welcoming and seeing the contents as ever changing actually allows us to sense the container of awareness, and it has always been there. This is good practice and is what it is really about. It is the big transformation, which all the main religions point to. For some, it is called Buddha Nature, others call it God, others refer to it as our true self, and others just call it peace.

THOUGHTS

I CAN'T STAND THIS ANYMORE

When I was living in a retreat center in north Wales between 2000 and 2005, we did quite a lot of meditation. In the early days, there was hard work. We would sit in meditation for forty to fifty minutes, depending on who was leading the retreat. We would have a ten-minute standing or walking break and then back on the cushion again.

Of course, it got tough, but I was going for enlightenment, so I was not going to let anything get in the way. I would sit there looking like a great meditator, like a spiritual warrior, perfectly still. Not just me, but twenty-five of us just sitting perfectly still and not making a sound. My knees would hurt, and my back would ache. At times, my knees would be screaming, but I wouldn't move. Not unless somebody else did first.

However, I had my moments. There were times when it was so bad that I would open one eye and glance over at the leader of the meditation, willing him to *ring that bell*. I just hoped nobody saw me do it. That would have been the end of all credibility, of course; after all, I had a reputation to think about. I would be sitting there thinking, "Why doesn't he just ring it? It must be fifty minutes now. It feels like hours. He is doing this on purpose. I know he is. What's the matter with him?" Off I would go, judging, commentating, and criticizing the teacher. Spinning. Spinning, spinning in my head. Of course, I would not tell anybody this. For all anybody knew, I was perfectly serene and untroubled by any of this.

For days and weeks, I would have these thoughts. There were several times when I would be thinking, "I can't stand this any longer. For **** sake, ring that bell. Are you an idiot, or what?"

However, something happened at around that time due to the very fact that the bell didn't ring when I wanted it to. Even though all those thoughts about not being able to stand it any longer were racing through my mind, I did stand it. I did not give up. What I mean is that I stopped taking my thoughts so seriously. I could see as clear as crystal that these thoughts were not telling me the truth. If I only listened to the thoughts, I would give up. However, I learned not to listen to them. What I listened to was the body. If the body showed me via the pain and aches, I could move because that was sensible. Even though at the time I was not always sensible.

There is a message in this for all of us. Stop listening to your thoughts, and listen to your body. The thinking mind is like a parrot; it just repeats what it has heard before. A parrot doesn't say anything original. It is not creative; it just churns out the same stuff day after day.

The thinking mind is a wonderful tool, but that is all. There is far more wisdom "behind" the thinking mind, but it is only when we stop taking it all so seriously that we can begin to hear it.

DIRTY CARS

IMAGINE YOU ARE sitting on a hillside, and before you is a road with cars going along both ways. You are enjoying yourself; you are at ease. You are just noticing all these lovely cars going one way and the other and minding your own business.

Then a thought occurs to you. I don't like some of those cars. Some of them also are dirtying the road. This is not good enough. So from the peacefulness of minding your own business, you march down to the road, stand right in the middle of the highway, and stop all the dirty cars. You wave them down. They stop and wind down their windows. You lean on the dirty car and talk to the driver. Please don't come along this road, you say; you are dirtying it. The driver responds, saying that she was going but you stopped her.

You do this time and again all day long. Stopping the cars, leaning in to windows, and asking them to leave.

Get it? Well, the cars are your thoughts. They enter and are about to leave, but you interrupt the process. Then you get upset, uptight, and miserable because you have a headful of thoughts. Not only that, because you stopped the cars and interfered with them leaving, you got dirtied by them by leaning on the side of the car. Leave them alone!

HAPPY BIRTHDAY

When we have a headful of thoughts, it can be really difficult to get some clarity. If we are angry, for example, it is very difficult to see what is really going on. We get taken over by thoughts, which, in turn, generate more emotion and so on.

When we are in the midst of emotional thinking, there is a technique that can help. I want you to repeat a phrase to yourself. A phrase that is real and that you can imagine yourself saying for real, such as a self-criticism or a criticism of somebody else. Something such as "He never does what he says he is going to do, never," or "I am useless. I always mess up." Repeat that to yourself for thirty seconds now and notice how it feels.

OK, now you will have noticed that although this is under test conditions, it was still unpleasant to repeat that phrase. Now I want you to say the phrase again, but this time, I want you to sing it to the tune of happy birthday. Do that for thirty seconds now.

OK, notice how it takes the seriousness out of it. I want you to use this when you are lost in emotionally charged thinking.

THE MIND IS LIKE A HAMMER

A SHORT WHILE ago, I woke up one Sunday morning after our village had been visited by a storm and noticed the felt had blown off the roof of our summer house. In usual Suryacitta style, I pretended it hadn't happened and went downstairs for a cup of tea.

Gaynor, my wife, woke up, witnessed the same thing, and, in true Gaynor style, didn't pretend it hadn't happened and sent me to the hardware store.

A few days later, I was hammering nails to refit the felt. Then a thought occurred to me: This hammer is a very useful tool for hammering nails. It is not much use for much else, such as baking bread or putting on wallpaper. In fact, we wouldn't even try. When we have finished with the hammer, however, it goes to rest in its toolbox. In other words, a hammer is useful for a certain task; then when the task is completed, it goes back into its toolbox to rest until the next time we need it.

Likewise, our thinking mind is a tool, a wonderful tool for thinking through something, planning, or problem solving. However, when we have finished using this tool, it is very different from the hammer. It won't go to rest until the next time we need it.

This tool just keeps on thinking—keeps hammering away—and whom does the thinking mind hammer? It hammers other people and us in the form of judgments, opinions, and criticisms. Sometimes all day long. The chattering mind is exhausting.

Often these thoughts leave us feeling cut off, afraid, anxious.

It doesn't have to be this way. We can have the great pleasure of a quiet mind.

What we need to do is to learn to cease believing all the thoughts that pass through our head. Believing all these thoughts is the fuel that keeps them alive.

An aspect of our mindfulness practice is to learn to allow thoughts to arise and allow them to pass away.

Practice this: Sit down for five minutes in a quiet space. The purpose of these next five minutes is simple:

to allow thoughts to arise and to notice when you cling to them then let them go. No matter what the thought is, let it go and turn your attention back to the here and now. This can be the breath, sounds, and your contact with the chair.

If we do a practice like this with regularity, then we can notice a little more space opening up inside and a little more ease entering into our life.

THE HEADY PROFESSOR

The professor of a local university went to see the local meditation master, Kendu. He wanted to learn meditation, and he could not think of a better way to learn than from a revered Zen master. He sat down and started to speak. He told Kendu about his work and about what he had discovered. He told the Zen master about his views on life, his beliefs, and even went on to tell him about what he thought was the meaning of life.

At some point, a young monk entered and brought them tea. Kendu started to pour the tea into the professor's cup. He poured and poured. The professor noticed the cup overflowing, but the master kept pouring. The professor spoke up and said, "Master, the cup is full, but you keep pouring. No more will go in!"

"This cup is like your mind, professor. Your mind is full—full of your own opinions and views about life. How can I show you Zen when your cup is full?"

I REALLY LIKE this story because it shows very beautifully that meditation is not about information. A head full of information about meditation can be as useless as no information. In fact, in most cases, it is worse than no information because if we have a lot of information about it, we think we know what it is.

You will never know what meditation really is just by having information about it. Just as you will never know the taste of an orange by reading about it. You need to bite into the orange, and then you know.

But this is only partly true. We don't ever get to know what meditation is because meditation is not a thing. We can say it is an activity to begin with, but then as we practice, we go beyond activity. We go beyond a technique into meditation proper. Where words fail us. We open to another dimension of being where there is no meditator, no meditation, but just…this. Just whatever is happening.

TAKING DOWN THE SCAFFOLDING OF THOUGHT

When I was living in the retreat center in north Wales, a large house about a mile away had scaffolding holding up its west wing, as it was leaning badly. The scaffolding, as I remember, had been there for many years and had done its job of holding it all together. Recently, in meditation, the image of that building and scaffolding popped into my mind, and I knew instantly the meaning of this.

It came to me that thoughts are like scaffolding; they hold things together. Sadly, for us, this is not always a pleasant experience. When I say thoughts, I am talking about the believed but unconscious thoughts that stampede through our heads all day long. I am not talking about conscious thinking around things such as planning a future event or reflection about a project. I am not talking either about creative thinking, which is a wonderful thing. The thoughts I am talking about are the stressful thoughts that race through our minds nearly all day long commenting on nearly all that we do. These thoughts keep repeating the same stories, and we keep believing those same stories—they keep our view of the world and ourselves fairly static from one day to the next. They are very predictable.

They keep in place our self-image, which without all these believed thoughts would just dwindle away to dust—but leaving us a whole lot more peaceful. Or more accurately, our self-image would be much more fluid and flexible, not tight and rigid.

When we are held together by thought scaffolding, we meet the world with preconceived ideas of how to act and be. These are based on experience, and they normally include fear and anxiety. For example, some of us get anxious when the phone rings. For others, it may be when they meet new people and they get shy or nervous. We all experience the consequences of thought scaffolding in slightly different ways.

Freeing ourselves from believed thoughts through mindfulness can be seen as taking away the scaffolding. Just as a scaffolder takes his or her time unscrewing the bolts that hold it all together, so the meditator takes his or her time becoming free of believed thoughts. It takes time to free ourselves from these believed thoughts because we feel without these "image-creating" thoughts, we would fall to pieces. Through mindfulness meditation, we can learn to trust in something that is "behind" and "beyond" this level of experience, and unless we learn this, we will always be held together by thought scaffolding. What that something "beyond" thought is cannot really be described—just experienced. But the best term I know is intuitive awareness.

Practice this: Find a quiet place and sit quietly for ten minutes. Take your attention to your breath and follow its rhythm. Notice when you get distracted by thoughts, but instead of criticizing yourself for getting lost in thinking, just say to yourself, "Thinking." When you have drifted into "thought land," there is always a moment when you "pop" back to awareness of here and now. At that moment, just again say to yourself, "Thinking," and return your attention to the body and the breath again. When this drifting happens, we often get into judgments about not doing it right and criticizing ourselves, but this is just tightening the thought scaffolding. We loosen the thought scaffolding simple by observing the thinking itself and not reacting in any way. This takes time, but once we begin to loosen the thought scaffolding, joy enters our life.

HELP, I CAN'T STOP THINKING!

ONE OF THE greatest contributors to distress and ill health and the biggest complaint from people in the courses and webinars I run is that of a busy mind. In the *Harvard Gazette, (see note 1 at end book)* research findings showed that 47 percent of our waking time is spent thinking about what is not going on. I tend to think it is actually more than 47 percent. If you don't believe me, try this later. While having a shower or drinking a cup of tea, make an aspiration to be fully present to the activity. You will be in for a surprise. Time and again, you will find yourself thinking about anything and everything. You will travel around the world; you will have all your work colleagues in the shower with you. You will be drinking tea with your local football team, or you will be arguing with your boss. Rarely will you be drinking your tea as well as knowing and experiencing drinking your tea.

Our tendency to get lost in thinking is powerful. I assume some of you have been fishing or at least have seen people fishing. They throw the bait and the hook into the water and wait. Along comes the fish, and it eats the bait and then bites onto the hook. It must hurt. The fish wriggles and tries to free itself from the hook, but the hook only goes deeper into the fish's mouth. Not only that, the fisher person then begins to reel the fish in. Not only has the fish got a hook in its mouth but also once out of the water, it cannot breathe.

The fish is now out of its natural environment—the water. This is similar in a way to us. Thoughts are like hooks; they come along and we bite onto them. Then we try to get free of them by criticizing ourselves or trying not to think, but this is a bad move. All those thoughts are just more hooks. We need to be able to simply unhook ourselves from the distressing thoughts, and it is both easier and more difficult than you think.

All these thoughts take us out of our natural environment, which is the present moment. Then we can enter into panic. We are lost; we are not at home in the body but swishing around on the end of a thought hook. Some thought hooks are easier to unhook from than others are. Some thoughts are what I call "fillers." They are not connected to our emotions particularly. They are just the chatter, which I deal with in other articles in this book. But some thought streams are powerful because they are connected to our emotions. Next,

I share in a meditation on how to deal with difficult emotional thinking.

Practice this—thought labeling: Think of an inner commentary that you would have in real life. It may be a criticism of yourself or somebody else. It may be a fear of something happening. For example, it may be something like, "I am useless; my life is a mess." Another example maybe something like, "He really hates me now; I know he does," or "She always does that; why doesn't she realize?" Make it real, and repeat it to yourself for twenty seconds. Do that now.

OK, so you will see even under these test conditions that thinking those thoughts is unpleasant. Even though we know it is an exercise, they still have an impact.

Now I want you to think the same thought stream again, but this time I want you to say before it the words "Having the thought..." You say the same thoughts as before but just put *having the thought* before you do. OK, do it now for thirty seconds.

So you will have noticed quite a difference. Putting *having a thought* before it gives you perspective and gives you distance from the thoughts. It allows you to see that it was just a thought and not a fact. I urge you to use the tool of thought labeling whenever you get lost in emotional thinking. When you have labeled the thought, return to the body and to the sensation in the body. Notice, label the thought, free yourself, and move on.

HELP, I CAN'T SLEEP EITHER!

THE TITLE FOR this section came to me while actually writing the book in Italy at the lovely Villa of Charles and Steve mentioned at the back of the book. I normally sleep very well with just the occasional sleepless night. However, one night while there, I awoke thinking about something we hadn't done for the business. I was spinning this way, and I was spinning that way. "Why haven't we sorted this with the bank? We are just wasting time and money. It is ridiculous." On and on I went. Then I realized what was happening. Upadana. In other words, I was hooked.

In the dead of night, things can seem very grave and serious. I knew I needed some perspective. So I decided to sing the whole phrase to myself to the tune of happy birthday. I did this, singing those very words to myself and then singing them out loud, which worked even better. After only a few times, I could gain perspective and let go of the hook. I was emotionally hooked into this whole thing about the bank, and I could feel the tension in my body. Singing it in this way made it lighter and far less serious. In the daytime, I could pursue it and sort it out.

Many people, including some friends and family, find it difficult to sleep. There may of course be a medical reason for this, and that needs to be checked out. However, mostly I believe this is not the case. What I say here will not be the whole story for some, but it may help.

If you run around all day being caught in the busy trap, not pausing, not taking a breather here and there, then you will pay the price. For instance, if you stay at your desk while eating lunch, then you will pay the price. Our mind and body need time away from doing, doing, doing. They need time to process what goes on. We need periods during the day when we stop the busyness, sit down, and sit still. This allows the body to process what has been happening.

The little upsets, the challenges, and stresses of life and work need time to be felt and worked through. If we don't give the mind and body time to do this while awake, then they will take the only opportunity they can—when our defenses are down—when we are asleep. When our defenses are down and something rises to the surface to be attended to, Upadana happens, and we get hooked.

So to help us sleep better, it may be worth looking not at our sleep but at our waking life. The clues are there. We need to resolve the unresolved issues in our lives while we are awake and allow sleep to resolve things in its own way. This is why we need an internal practice. A time we spend alone or quietly. It may be a walk for some, it may be painting for others, and it may be meditation for the likes of many others and me.

Watch out for the busy trap.

FEELINGS

PUSHING OUR BUTTONS

IT IS VERY easy for someone to come along and push our buttons. They may criticize us, look at us the wrong way, or just ignore us. We can feel that very deeply. Others know where our soft spot is, and they stab their finger right where we don't want them to. This may be intentional or not; it doesn't always matter that much. However, they tend to take their finger off the button very quickly; in other words, they say the remark or walk past us, which lasts a few seconds, then off they go.

What happens next though is very interesting. They take their finger off the button, but then what do we do with our finger? You guessed it; we put our finger on exactly the same spot they did. But what is different is that we keep it on far longer than they were capable of. They have gone off now enjoying a glass of wine or a game of tennis. But we are too busy pressing our button. We keep our finger on the button through one way and one way only. With our thinking. We ruminate; we dwell on what happened. We go over and over it again: "I should have said this," or "I should have said that." Over and over again, we dig around, hurting ourselves in the process. We imagine that somehow all this thinking, or rather overthinking, will help. It never does.

What we need to do is to take our finger off the button. This means we label our thinking as just that, thinking. We need to notice that we are lost in our head. Then when that is done, we can take our attention to the feeling in the body. It may be anger, or it may be shame or embarrassment. It may be sadness, frustration, or guilt. It doesn't matter. All our emotions, no matter what, are made of two components: thoughts and sensations in the body. I have looked for many years and never found an experience outside of these two components. This makes it simple to know how to proceed, but not necessarily easy.

Our tendency is to want to overthink, but we must resist this by labeling our thoughts as thoughts. Locate the sensation in the body, and then notice what it feels like. Is it soft, hard, or whatever? Be interested in it. Before you know it, the sensation has decreased in intensity.

The reason we don't stay in the chattering mind here is that those types of thoughts are the fuel for the emotion. Emotion or feeling is the fire and the believed thoughts are the fuel. We need to starve the emotion of what keeps it alive: thoughts.

However, be aware that our addiction to thinking is very strong, so you need to do this over and over again.

ANXIETY—IS IT TRUE OR FALSE?

FOR A FEW years, I used to feel anxious every autumn; mostly I used to just pretend it wasn't there and try to ignore it, as is my way. If something needs doing, I tend to put it off until tomorrow.

However, the anxiety was trying to tell me something. It was knocking on the door, saying, "Suryacitta, you need to do your tax returns before it is too late." At some point when they couldn't be put off any longer, I would do the tax returns, and the anxiety would be replaced by relief. The problem being is that I am not very good at sums and accounts, but in the end, I managed to do them. Now it is much easier as the accountant does them. Thank the universe for accountants.

The anxiety I was experiencing is what I would call true anxiety. It has a purpose, and it is trying to help me. It makes me feel uncomfortable so that I will act. Very wise when you think about it; however, there is a big difference between true anxiety mentioned earlier and what I would call "false anxiety."

Let's look a little more closely. True anxiety has its source in the external world, or more accurately, in reality. I really did need to get the accounts done; if not, then I would face the consequences. With true anxiety, we can do something; we can act, and then the anxiety can diminish. This sort of anxiety is actually our wisdom letting us know something.

False anxiety has its source not in reality but in our head. It is created by the spinning thoughts that go around and around. We can so easily fall into false anxiety. We may get a phone call or hear a rumor that we may lose our job. There is an external factor here, but what we do is go into overthinking: "I'll never get another job. That's it. My career is ended," or "How on earth will I manage? Nobody is going to give me another job. I can't stand this. It is a nightmare."

We spin, spin, spin. This is the second dagger (for an explanation of the daggers, see the section titled "The Two Daggers"). The first dagger is the phone call or the rumor; the second dagger is our storyline about it. It is out of control, and we believe all our thoughts. We need to get out of our thoughts and into reality. It may be that you are going to lose your job, but all this overthinking is just tortuous.

All this spinning about our predicament is very different from sitting down and reflecting on the situation. I am not going to say you will feel good about the whole thing, but at least you will not be using the second dagger. The second dagger is always done with our unconscious thinking, our spinning. When we come out of the spinning head, which just creates more anxiety, we can then see more clearly. We can think and reflect about the best way forward. On a webinar recently, a woman realized that underneath all her thinking was a low-level anxiety in her chest. But all the thinking kept her from noticing this. She was able to experience this anxious sensation in her chest and to "listen" to it. Be attentive to it.

MELTING THE ICE

In one of her books, the late and great teacher Charlotte Joko Beck used the image of ice cubes to describe human beings.

Imagine an ice cube two feet long and twelve inches wide with spindly little legs and arms. This, she says, is an image of most human beings. We are like blocks of ice going about our lives. We are ice because we have frozen out our real sensitivity and vulnerability to the world. We go through life bumping into other blocks of ice. When in a disagreement, we often try to bump the other blocks of ice so that they will shatter first.

Some of us try to appear soft by trying to be nice or agreeable, but underneath that, we are still ice. The ice is there because we are afraid of our softness and vulnerability. Being an ice cube is familiar and feels kind of safe, but it is a cold and lonely life.

Awareness and meditation are ways of melting the ice. This is what we must do. We must begin the long and gradual melting of the ice that keeps us from truly living our life.

We need to observe ourselves; we need to begin to live in the body and not exist in our thoughts. We cannot use effort to melt the ice; it can only be done through awareness and through experiencing ourselves this very moment.

It is good to know what the ice is made from. Primarily it is created by and maintained by our deeply held beliefs and about how life should be. It is a protection against feeling the realities of life. It is maintained by the need to be *right*. We remain a block of ice when we refuse to see how we mistreat other people and ourselves, with judgments, criticisms, and almost constantly avoiding our more difficult emotions.

In meditation, we melt the ice by experiencing the body and all its tensions and sensations—pleasant and unpleasant. Each moment of feeling something in the body begins the process of melting.

In daily life, we need to begin to observe how we are with other people. How we want to control some people, to please other people. How we bristle when somebody looks at us the wrong way or don't compliment us when we think they should.

Our capacity to observe ourselves with honesty begins the melting process. At some point, we will notice that we are not quite as anxious as we used to be, or we are more patient with other people and ourselves. As we melt and become a little mushier, we may notice that our relationships are more satisfying.

However, it is not always pain free. As we melt and come to know ourselves, we may have to make some decisions, which are painful for us and other people. Some acquaintances we may see that we have to let go of, or we acknowledge that a certain job just isn't good for us.

This is the path of awareness and the melting of the ice. It brings with it responsibility of our life, and some of us just don't want that sort of responsibility.

It is good to realize, however, that being an ice cube is not our natural state. We have created this state to protect ourselves, to protect our soft center. As the transformation gets underway and the melting begins, we begin to sense our real nature, which is water. In water, there is movement and life, but in ice, all life is suspended until the melting takes place.

As we melt, other people who meet us will begin to be warmed by us and may begin to melt too if there is a certain amount of receptivity.

Melting the ice is not always easy but is the path to joy.

NOT RUNNING AWAY ANYMORE

People often ask me about my time living in a meditation retreat center where I lived for five years. Some people think they could never do that. Others think that it was an easy option, and it is running away from real life.

Well, let me tell you that it is where I stopped running away. Living that simple lifestyle was a pleasure for my personality and me, but it was also where I stopped running and turned around and faced myself.

We are always running away. The slightest discomfort and off we go. We go to the movies and we go shopping. We overeat, overachieve, and overwork just to avoid the discomfort and insecurity about life.

One of our favorite ways to avoid this discomfort is to overthink. Think, think, think—that's what we do all day long. We think about anything and everything. You think so that you don't have to feel the anxious tremble and the center of your being.

When I first moved to Leicestershire in the United Kingdom, I was asked what I did for a living. I told him that I sit on my bottom doing absolutely nothing and teach people how to do just the same. He looked at me and said, "Is that all? Sounds like an easy way to make a living."

I invited him to come on a day retreat with me. That was in 2007, and he still has not attended.

Sitting still is scary for some people. It is when the anxious tremble can be felt most clearly. Only when we face this deeply held anxious feeling and restlessness can we begin to embrace it and gradually be at ease in our life. So stop running away and sit down.

Practice this: Each morning for the next seven days, make an aspiration to turn toward that unease and restlessness when you become aware of it. Take a few minutes several times a day just to be still and feel it. Locate it in the body, and notice what it feels like. Observe the qualities of it. Then get on with your day.

UPADANA – DO I DO THAT?

"Upadana" is not a word you will be familiar with, but you do it every day. Loosely translated, the Sanskrit word means something like getting hooked, clinging to, or attached to. Upadana is the cause of our suffering.

Upadana is that state of clinging when we are locked into a negative state of mind. Or when we are locked into chasing after something that is pleasurable. Let us suppose we are walking in the park enjoying the trees and sunshine. Then a thought appears or we see something that reminds us of an event. You see a tree similar to the one you used to have near your home with your ex-partner. "What happened between us?" you begin to ponder. "We were so in love, and then it all went pear shaped very quickly."

You begin to remember all the lovely things you did and perhaps some of the difficult things you went through.

Then, feeling lonely, you wonder, "Will I ever meet anybody ever again?" Before you know it, you are feeling depressed or at least sad.

What happened? Upadana is what happened. You got hooked into your thinking, and off you went. All those thoughts fueled and increased the feeling of loneliness, and you got lost in the story.

You were in your drama, and we cling to own drama. We cling to it because it makes us feel we are the center of the universe. It gives us a sense of who we are and our place in the world. It doesn't matter to us if it is a place better than most or lower than most. We are desperate to have a place and to know it.

What do we need to do? We need to be willing to come out of the drama, out of the story in our heads. We need to leave our thought-made world and come back home to the body. Remember, the body is our home, so that is where we need to be. We need to become aware of and to experience the sense of loneliness without the story. If we can do this for just a few minutes, we will find that the feeling of loneliness begins to be very bearable indeed.

THREE STEPS TO WORKING WITH UPADANA

1. Stop and acknowledge that you are hooked and clinging.
2. Come out of the storyline. Staying in the story fuels the negative emotion. It is like pouring fuel on the fire.
3. Let go, move on, and have a good day.

DOG SHIT, TRANSFORMATION, AND THE PLUM TREE

MEDITATION IS ALL about transformation. It transforms us from a life of agitation and confusion to a life of ease and clarity. But we have to know how this transformation works. It doesn't work by *trying* to transform ourselves. It doesn't work by us wishing we were different. When I think about how most people go about trying to change themselves, I think of the elastic band scenario.

We find ourselves a certain way, with certain foibles and habits, which we don't like. We would rather be different; we would rather not have these habits and ways of being. But it is as if we were an elastic band. In other words, we try to stretch ourselves to be different. I am like this, but I want to be like that. So we try and try and try to mold and stretch ourselves to try to be that way. But just like when you stretch an elastic band far enough, either it snaps or when you let go it just returns to its original shape.

If we try to be different than we are, we always end up back at square one, just like the elastic band. We do not change through effort.

Gaynor and I live near a beautiful park. One day after leading a retreat, I was walking in the park, and I stepped in some dog shit. I grimaced, cursed, and eventually wiped it off on the grass. When I got back, I put my shoe underneath the outdoor tap and washed the remainder off. It was satisfying to get the last bit off.

Dog shit is definitely something we don't want around. But we have a plum tree in our garden. If I had put the dog shit underneath the plum tree, what would Gaynor and I be eating next year? Plums of course. But these plums would be made partly from dog shit along with rotten leaves, dead insects, and other rotten stuff we don't want.

Nature knows how to transform dog shit into sweet-tasting plums. It knows how to transform all dead and smelly things into beautiful-looking flowers and plants. It doesn't have a problem with the dog shit; we do.

We all have the equivalent of dog shit in our lives—those foibles, bad habits, and difficulties that we don't like and definitely don't want. However, we don't do what nature does. Nature allows the dead things to be exposed to the earth and bingo! Transformation happens.

How then do we transform our habits and difficulties? How do we do what nature does so well? Well, transformation happens when we acknowledge, accept, and experience all those parts of ourselves we don't want.

We learn to turn toward difficulties and to feel the sadness, the anxiety, the vulnerability, or whatever and allow the light of experience and awareness to transform these experiences. We just need to set up the conditions and it will happen. The right conditions are curiosity as to what is going on, acknowledgment of what is there, acceptance of what is there, and allowance of yourself to feel what is there. To give it space and attention.

We don't need to do anything else. Nature will take care of the rest, and before we know it, what we thought was dog shit is actually sweet-tasting plums…and always has been.

Practice this: Sit down, and be curious about what is going on for you right now. If there is some discomfort, take your attention there, and acknowledge it. Accept fully what is here right now. Notice what it feels like, give it space, and let it be. No need to try and change it or zap it with healing lights. Just feel it. Listen to it. If you get lost in the storyline, let the thoughts go and come back into the body. Notice the different qualities of this. Hard, soft, trembly, scared. Just stay with it, and be curious.

This is not just how we become comfortable with difficult experiences but also how we allow them to transform. What we feel, we heal. It is nature's way.

YOUR REAL HOME

Most of us are fortunate to have a home. A home ideally is a place of comfort and safety—where we can relax. We can return from work or a trip out and enjoy the freedom that being at home often brings.

If you are anything like my wife, Gaynor, and me, you will also enjoy leaving home occasionally and going on holiday.

Gaynor and I, though, no matter how much we have enjoyed our time away, are always pleased to return home.

When we return home, we have a look around the house and check on various rooms just to make sure all is well, no leaky roofs, no break-ins, and so on. Gaynor, too, always checks around the garden, making sure everything is OK. It is a way of just checking in again with our home.

However, we all have another home in which we spend very little time at.

Stop reading now and take few moments to think what I could be referring to.

This other home I am referring to is our body, or we could say the present moment. However, we often don't want to be at home in the body or in the present moment.

But why would this be?

Well, instead of being here with life as it is in our own body, we tend to want to fantasize or worry about the future and the past. We have a life happening here and now, but we spend most of it thinking about a different one. Often a one that is either better or worse than our real one.

If you pay attention to yourself during the day, you will notice just how much you are lost in anxious thinking, wishful thinking, problem solving, planning, blaming, and a whole lot more.

Of course, there are things we need to think about sometimes, such as planning a trip or working out a strategy for work, but this is functional thinking. In other words, we are using the mind to do something useful.

However, most of the time, the mind just churns out stories, opinions, judgments, and criticisms that we have no control over.

Through mindfulness, we begin to notice this tendency for the mind to chatter, chatter, chatter.

Depending on the nature of the chatter, life can be very painful.

THE SEARCH AND WHAT'S DRIVING IT

In your more honest moments, you will admit that you are constantly searching for something—let us call it happiness or peace of mind. Perhaps the promotion with a great pension will do it. Maybe Mr. or Miss Right will. Maybe if I work hard, people will admire me, and that will do it. Perhaps if I change myself enough, that will bring me peace of mind.

We are forever searching for what we believe will stop the distress or will bring that peace we want so much. But we need to do this differently. We need to see what is driving the search. We need to uncover and to learn to be with the underlying distress, that deep trembling anxiety that is deep within each of us. But we don't want to. In fact, it is the last thing we want to do. We want to keep on dreaming that someday we will make it. In our practice, there is little place for dreaming.

Dreaming is for people who are asleep. We need to wake up. We need to wake up to what is driving our searching for something to fill this hole we feel. Something to placate the inadequacy we feel at the center of our life. This sense of lack is what fuels our life. If you don't believe me, then sit down for thirty minutes without doing anything at all and notice the edginess you feel. Observe how you want to do anything but to be here with yourself and the simplicity of just being here with yourself. You are restless. I am restless. We are restless, and we are afraid to stop because when we stop we are faced with this underlying sense of edginess, dis-ease, and fear.

Our searching is a way of avoiding this very place. At some point, if we practice well, we realize that searching is not really helping. It is just living in hope that something will happen. That somehow, we will be zapped by the universe and we will find peace of mind. I am afraid there is no zapping. Once we begin to give up the search and turn our attention around, something begins to shift. Over time we sense that we are running less and are a little less anxious and afraid. This is the shift that needs to happen if we are to find the peace we so desire.

A MINDFUL LIFE

WE THINK TOO much, want too much, and rush too much. This section explores our everyday life. We often don't want to be with the ordinary things in life, such as stirring porridge, walking up the stairs, or doing the ironing. We tend to want to rush through these activities to get to the "real" stuff. This is the real stuff. This book and the Mindful Life program, which I have developed and you can read about at the end of the book, and includes live webinars with myself, are about turning these often-mundane activities to times of satisfaction and quiet joy.

TEXTING OR NEXTING

One day I was sitting in a traffic jam in a city in the United Kingdom, which, let me tell you, is a common thing in my country, when I noticed to my left on the pavement a woman walking along and texting.

Nothing wrong with this of course, and there is no judgment here of the woman, as most of us do this, but what I also noticed is that she was leaning forward and rushing. Which again most of us do.

Walking and texting is quite a common sight in most countries nowadays and may not be a cause for concern. However, maybe because I had nothing else to do, I started to ponder on this. It was not the texting that was the most remarkable thing but the fact that she seemed to be leaning forward, almost leaning forward into the future.

I pondered the word "texting," a strange word when you repeat it to yourself. But then the word "nexting" came to mind. Not only do we spend time texting, but we also spend time nexting.

This means our attention is rarely in the here and now but in what is coming next. We can be so easily lost in the future. I think most of us spend most of our time nexting. "Next" implies the future, which is to come but is not here yet. If you pay attention and are honest with yourself, you will notice that most of the time you are nexting. When we are not, then often we may be lost in the past.

I don't mean that texting is wrong or bad or anything like that. What I mean is that a lot of our activities are done because we are incapable of being in the present. We are slaves to doing.

Many people come to me about the cause of stress, and I must say the cause is very simple.

We have too many thoughts in our heads telling us all sorts of things need doing. These thoughts are constantly pulling us out of the present moment. If you don't believe, follow the short exercise at the end of this anecdote.

One of the exercises I give to my students on the courses I run is to notice during the day when you are lost in nexting. Then I ask them to bring their mind back into the present moment to whatever they are doing in the here and now.

A lot of them are surprised at just how much they live not only in their heads, which is where it appears that thinking takes place, but also in their thoughts about the future and past.

Practice this: Put down this book and sit quietly with eyes either open or closed. Now just sit and don't do anything. Don't text, don't read, no need to plan, no need to reflect on anything at all. Just sit and observe what happens. Be honest with yourself. Notice after a while the urge to think about something, anything, but just being here and now in the simplicity of this moment. Observe the thoughts and feel the impulses and urges to get up and do something. See if you can do this for the first ten minutes. Then take awareness into your everyday life. Notice how you want to rush through things to get to the next thing—nexting. No need to judge or criticize yourself; just observe yourself.

WHO'S THIS IN THE SHOWER WITH ME?

When you start living a mindful life, you soon realize that you are not living a mindful life. When I first started to practice meditation and mindfulness I soon realized that I was rarely here doing what I was doing. Let me explain.

I like listening to music. I remember when I was keen on the rock group Queen and listening to them quite a lot. I remember though realizing that I could not listen to a whole track without drifting off to other things, so I did an experiment. I said to myself that I would try and listen to a whole track without thinking about something else.

So I lay on my floor in the house with my headphones on. Here we go, I thought, a whole track without getting lost in distraction. After less than a minute, *bing*! I realized that I had just been talking to a clown (I saw on TV the previous day) about how hot he gets in his suit. So I turned my attention back to the music and really paid attention. Less than thirty seconds later, *bing*! I realized that I had drifted off. This time I was going over an argument with an old friend, which we had never even had. This happened again and again over the six minutes of music. This was ridiculous.

I realized that my mind was restless and that I could not even listen to a six-minute music track without traveling the world or dwelling on my problems, most of which I didn't have anyway. I would be going over conversations in my head, planning things that had already happened, and pondering things that were clearly never going to happen.

I did realize later when I started going to meditation classes that I was not alone. Not only that, I realized that a restless mind is universal.

In the courses I run, I ask people to notice when they are engaged in everyday activities such as drinking coffee, walking up the stairs, and doing the washing up and to notice just how often they drift away. They soon come to realize even though they are washing the dishes with their body, their mind is doing something else. For some this can come as quite a surprise at just how much necessary thinking goes on.

A few years ago, I had a small wager with a friend that Chelsea football club would win the Champions League; after all, they had one of the best managers in the world. One particular match, they were playing at home, and the team they were playing had a player sent off. They lost the match; they were out of the Champions League. They had lost at home to ten men.

The next morning, I was having a shower, and lo and behold, the then Chelsea manager Jose Mourinho turns up uninvited into my shower. I prefer to shower alone, of course, but there you go. I started telling him off. "How could you lose at home to a side from Spain who had ten men? The team was useless." I told him where he had gone wrong and how he should have approached the game.

Then *bing*! I realized what I was doing. Jose Mourinho hadn't entered the shower uninvited; I had invited him in. I let him leave and then decided that while I was in the shower I may as well have one.

How often though do we do this? How often are we doing an activity only to find we are mentally engaged in a different one? Living a mindful life is the beginning of noticing this and learning to be present with what we are doing. The present moment is where we eventually find the joy we have been searching for all our lives.

Practice this: Next time you shower or have a bath, notice who you invite in with you. Notice the conversations you have with him or her. Notice the places you travel to in the world. Observe all this and then return to what you are doing. Learn to feel the heat and the water on the skin. We can be alive to the simple activity of having a shower…alone.

LOOKING FOR THE KEY

Billy is staggering home late one night. He had one or two drinks too many but is in a good mood after a great night with his mates. When he gets to his door, he cannot find his keys. However, he does vaguely remember dropping them earlier.

He begins looking for them underneath the lamppost. He gets on his hands and knees and searches in the grass, under the shrubs, in the hedge. At that point, his mate Fred comes along, also staggering from a few too many.

"Billy, my good friend, what are you doing down there?" asks Fred.

Billy replies, "I lost my keys and I am looking for them."

"Oh well, let me help you," responds Fred. So Fred gets down on his hands and knees and helps look for Billy's keys.

Half an hour passes, and Fred asks, "Billy, my dear old mate, I cannot find your keys here. Where did you lose them?"

"Oh," replies Billy, "I lost them in the back garden."

"You lost them in the back garden?" shouts Fred. "So why on earth are we looking here in the front garden?"

"Because the light is better here under the lamppost."

I LOVE THIS story because it is so ridiculous. But we can ask ourselves if we are much different from Billy. Billy was looking where the light was best, but of course, it was all in vain; the keys were not there.

We too are looking for something, and that something I am going to call happiness, peace, contentment, joy. Call it whatever you want, as these words point to the same thing.

However, this is where we are similar to Billy. We are looking in the wrong place. Where do we look for happiness? Relationships, possessions, jobs, children, promotion. These are the more obvious places where we look; however, there are other "places" we look too. A good or bad reputation depending on what we think will make us special. We want approval and to be noticed or not noticed depending on our conditioning.

I am not saying we should not have any of these, of course, but what I am saying is that they will not bring the happiness we seek. They can bring much pleasure and satisfaction, of course, but they are limited in what they can bring.

They are limited in what they can bring because they are subject to change and uncertainty. So to be truly happy, we need to be at ease with these facts of life.

IS THAT SO?

There was once an old farmer who lived a simple life with his son. One day his horse ran away. Upon hearing the news, his neighbors came to visit. "Such bad luck," they said, feeling for the farmer.

"Is that so?" the farmer replied.

The next morning, the horse returned, bringing with it three other wild horses. "How wonderful," the neighbors said.

"Is that so?" replied the old farmer.

The following day, his son tried to ride one of the untamed horses. He was thrown off, and he broke his leg. The neighbors again came to offer their sympathy for the fall.

"Is that so?" answered the farmer. The day after, military officials came to the village to draft young men

into the army. Seeing that the son's leg was broken, they passed him by. The neighbors congratulated the farmer on how well things had turned out.

"Is that so?" replied the farmer.

OFTEN WHEN SOMETHING happens, we like to judge the incident as either good or bad. If it is an unfortunate event, we can so easily go into, "This is it; my life is ruined." If we can just step back from the whole thing, which at first is not easy, then we can have a greater perspective on the events that happen in our life. Supposing we get a call from our boss saying we are being made redundant. Our usual reaction is to go into panic or blame or perhaps to feel sorry for ourselves. "I will never get another job." We tell ourselves.

But if we can just take that step back, breathe, and not go into the storyline, we just may be able to say to ourselves, "Let's see, what do I really need to do here?" This is wisdom because we are beginning to see one of the simplest but profound truths of life: everything changes.

RETRO MINDFULNESS—THE FORGOTTEN ART OF PAUSING

MOST PEOPLE WILL remember or be familiar with vinyl albums, aka long-playing records. If you were not around when they were, then you will probably know about them. They are apparently making a comeback.

I used to sell secondhand records in the early 1980s when I was a trader, so I remember them very fondly indeed. Vinyl albums normally have six or seven tracks on both sides. When you played them, there was a pause in between each track, nothing except the occasional crackle. The next track would play, then another pause, a gap before the next one.

Then around the middle of the 1980s, CDs came out. I remember thinking at the time that the pauses, the space between the tracks, were shorter than albums. However, I didn't think I was onto something really significant and forgot all about it. Now we have digital music, and lo and behold, we have music without any pauses, without any gaps between the tracks.

So all those years ago, I was onto something significant. What I mean is the change from albums, to CDs, and from CDs to digital represents another change. A change in both our minds and our lives. In the days of vinyl albums, I believe our lives had more pauses in them; our minds had more space in them. It seems nowadays that most people are so very busy that their lives are full of activity, and their minds are full of constant chatter.

This leads to a very restless existence for most of us. If we have a busy mind, we will have a busy life. If you have a busy life, you will have a busy mind. I am not talking about genuine work here but the tendency to remain busy or being restless. For example, even when the job is done, we look for the next thing to occupy us. It may be calling a friend, cleaning the car, e-mailing, and texting. Anything at all as long as we don't stop and experience ourselves.

Blaise Pascal, the French philosopher, said that the root of human problems is that we cannot sit quietly in a room by ourselves. That was in the seventeenth century. How much truer today, I wonder.

I often begin my mindfulness courses by talking about this very thing. I have an old album as a prop. I make sure we don't rush through the material just to fill our heads with information. Like the album, we pause—we have gaps in our sessions. Gaps where there is just silence like the gaps between the tracks. Mindfulness is not only about information but also about practice. We have breaks, and even during the teaching, we will have pauses and silence. I give a teaching, I present an idea, and then we will be quiet, allowing the idea to percolate. Initially people find this a little odd, but it is surprising how they come to appreciate it.

Teaching is like throwing a pebble into a pond. We throw in a pebble, and often we throw in another pebble before that has settled and another. In this way, the mud never settles, and the pond remains cloudy. But if we wait a while, allow the idea to be absorbed, then it can be understood and hopefully make a difference to a person's life because he or she has absorbed it.

So what do we need to do about this? Well, we need to go retro. We need to bring pauses and space back into our lives. Our minds and bodies are not made to be on the go constantly. So, if possible, learn to pause during the day. Not to achieve something or attain something but just because it is good for us.

Practice this: One way of doing this is to just ask yourself, "What is happening right now?" This question is like turning on a light switch. Notice your breath, feel your breath. Particularly the end of the out breath. Lengthen the out breath by a second or two. Just feel it come, and feel it go. You can do this for as little as thirty seconds or sit down and do it for three minutes. You can even do it on the go if you cannot stop what you are doing.

Doing this several times a day can help bring just a little more sanity and clarity into our lives.

THE MEDITATION MASTER AND THE VASE

Recently I noticed how irritated I was becoming with our new printer, which seemed incapable of doing the most basic of things, like printing. This got me thinking about my relationship to my possessions. I lived for five years with very few possessions while living in a Buddhist retreat center, and I must say, I was very happy indeed. I rarely missed the *things* of this world.

One of my reflections has been that it is not really about possessions but about my relationship to my possessions that matters.

I am reminded of Hakuin, the meditation master, who was ninety years old and who decided to visit his old friend Basho in the next valley. Basho was also ninety years old. They had been friends since they were eight years old. They entered monastic life together as children and trained together for decades. He gathered all his monks and nuns together and told them that he intended to go see his dear old friend Basho. He told them neither his friend nor he had long to live and it was time for them to see each other one last time. He asked them to look after each other in his absence and to practice well.

They had a wonderful time together, reminiscing and joking, but all things must end, and it was time for Hakuin to head back to his own monastery.

Hakuin had a very devoted housekeeper. Hakuin, though he could be very stern when he needed to be, had always been very kind to her and her family. She loved him very much.

She realized that Hakuin was due back and thought to herself that she wanted to prepare his room for his arrival. She swept the floor, cleaned his worktops, and polished his ornaments. Then she saw his favorite vase. This vase had been handed down by his master and the masters before him. It was very precious indeed. Each morning, after his meditation, he caressed the vase and remembered his beloved masters.

She picked up the vase, began cleaning it, and then dropped it; it smashed into a hundred pieces.

At that moment, the handle of the door to the room began to move. Hakuin walked in, and she looked at him in horror, ready to apologize. However, he looked at her in the eyes and said, "Don't you worry, my dear. I got that vase for pleasure, not for pain."

Maybe we could ponder on our relationship to our own possessions. Maybe it is worth asking, "Do my possessions bring me pleasure, or do they bring me pain?" Perhaps we can learn to be happy with possessions and happy without them.

A CRACK IN IT

The Buddhist master sat and surveyed his students. One of them then stood up, bowed, and asked him a question. "Please, master, can you tell us how we should view our life?"

He sat quietly for a few moments and then reached for a beautiful vase on the table next to him. "See this vase," he said. "It has a crack in it." Nobody could see the crack, but he insisted it was there. They were confused.

He said, "Someday, this vase will break. It will fall apart. That is the crack in it. So we have to be mindful when holding it. We have to treat it with care.

"If it were a plastic vase, you wouldn't care for it in the same way because it wouldn't break so easily.

"Likewise, we have a crack in us. It is called our future death. Our relationships have a crack in them.

At some point, our loved ones will leave us, or we will leave them. That is why our relationships are precious."

"We need to cherish ourselves and each other because just like the vase, we are precious and easily broken."

THERE ARE MANY cracks in our lives. The wonderful poet and singer/songwriter Leonard Cohen once said, "Everything has a crack in it. It is where the light gets in."

We should look for these cracks because they are our portal to the land of happiness. When we feel vulnerable, this is a crack. Our usual sense of our solid self is being shaken. This vulnerable "anxious quiver" should be welcomed and felt in the body; however, most of the time, we do what we can to avoid it—what a shame!

These "anxious quivers" can happen when we have been criticized. Being criticized means our sense of who we are is being challenged.

If we can turn toward these moments of vulnerability or the ending of things, then we begin to sense something new. Our sense of ourselves begins to become more fluid and more flexible.

This turning toward the feeling of vulnerability begins to bring us into an intimate relationship with the whole of life and ourselves. We begin to intuitively see that each moment of our life is precious because it is all we have. There is nothing outside of this moment except our thoughts that there is something better in some other time and place.

Our mindfulness practice helps us to see this for ourselves, not just as an idea but also as a living reality.

We begin to see what the master was saying, that every event, every relationship, every moment has a crack in it, and because of this crack, it is precious.

Practice this: Take your seat in meditation. Feel the contact with the chair or cushions. Sense your hands resting in your lap. After a few minutes, begin to feel your breath. Really feel it. Now pay particular attention to the beginning of the in breath and the end of the out breath.

Allow yourself to feel emotionally what it means to breathe. In this breath is reflected the whole of life, that everything has a beginning and an end. Allow yourself to feel this. Now pay particular attention to the end of the out breath. Notice what it feels like to let go on this breath. Is there a little holding on—is there any "emotional holding" of the breath as it ends?

Spend a few minutes in this space, and allow any resistance or fears to be felt.

Now release your awareness of the breath, and reflect that just as the breath has a beginning and an end, so do all your relationships. This is not about becoming depressed but about learning to cherish each other.

Welcome any feelings of sadness or joy or whatever arises. Just turn toward these feelings, and embrace them.

If it gets too much, then stop and give yourself a break.

This is a way of learning to view each moment as precious.

THE DIFFERENCE BETWEEN HEAVEN AND HELL

A very angry samurai warrior was looking around the monastery. He opened the door to the meditation hall and saw a little old monk sitting in meditation. "Monk," he shouted, "tell me the difference between heaven and hell, or I will cut off your head."

"Go to hell, you dirty, stupid man." The samurai was not used to being spoken to like that; people were normally frightened of him. He walked up to the little Zen monk, fuming, and lifted his sword to cut off his head. At that moment, the Zen monk looked up and said, "That is hell, my young friend." The samurai froze. He realized that the little monk had risked his life not to tell him the difference between heaven and hell but to show him.

Tears came to the face of the samurai, who let go of his sword and dropped to his knees in front of the little monk. "And that is heaven, my friend."

HEAVEN AND HELL are not places we go to but states of mind we inhabit. Anger, ill will, jealousy, envy, and craving are all hellish states of mind. Kindness, compassion, connection, gentleness, and courage are heavenly states of mind.

How do we move from hell to heaven? We do it through daily practice of awareness. We get there by learning to treat ourselves with kindness instead of criticism. But this is easier said than done. We have spent many years treating ourselves harshly. It takes time; it takes patience. Again and again we see how we get lost in our thought-made world, and we return to the here and now. When we return to the here and now, which is the body and its senses, we soften. We harden when we get lost in our heads, but we soften when we come into the body.

THE ROOTS OF MINDFULNESS

MINDFULNESS, AS WE know it today, has its origins within the Buddhist tradition. It did not just spring out of fresh air into today's busy world. It has been practiced for many, many centuries, at least for two thousand five hundred years.

The Buddha taught how to use our attention to free us from mental and emotional suffering. He called this way of paying attention Sati, which has been translated into "mindfulness." My own definition is this: *Mindfulness is knowing what is happening, while it is happening non-judgmentally, and knowing the mind's perception of what is happening.*

Mindfulness, then, has a purpose, and that purpose is to end our suffering or at least to alleviate our self-inflicted suffering. This was the Buddha's great insight. He knew how to end suffering. The basic Buddhist teachings from which mindfulness grew are called the Four Noble Truths of life.

THE FOUR TRUTHS OF LIFE

1. The Buddha's first insight into life is that there is some suffering or at least dissatisfaction in life.
2. The cause of suffering—a kind of clinging—is on many different levels. Possessions, people, ideas, reputation, views, beliefs, self-image.
3. There is an end to suffering.
4. The path to the end suffering.

FIRST TRUTH: THERE IS FRUSTRATION

Now let's get practical and see how we create suffering or, more accurately, how I created suffering on a few particular occasions.

When I first started meditating in the late 1980s, I was living back with my parents for a few months. We had three rooms downstairs: kitchen/dining room, what we called the living room, and another that we called the front room. I would meditate in the front room. I would sit early in the morning, normally undisturbed, and again in the evening, not quite so undisturbed. This particular time, I was sitting in meditation in the front room and really enjoying it. I was feeling very, very spiritual indeed.

I remember being very quiet, very still in my very important meditation—then it happened. From the living room next door, where my mum was sitting, I heard it. I heard the sound—the sound was the theme tune to *Coronation Street*. *Coronation Street*, for those who don't know, is a very popular soap opera in the United Kingdom.

I went in a fraction of a second from a peaceful meditator to a very grumpy meditator. I started to huff and puff. I moaned to myself. I wound myself up, complaining about my lovely mum just watching her favorite TV program. I shouldn't have to put up with this, I thought. Here I am trying to meditate, and I have to listen to that. These were thoughts running through my mind. I felt frustrated that *my* meditation had been disturbed by something as mundane as the theme music to *Coronation Street*. People, including my mum, were clearly not as evolved as I was.

This is a simple example of the first truth; there is dissatisfaction here in the form of frustration.

SECOND TRUTH: THE CAUSE OF FRUSTRATION

It seems at first glance at this that the cause of my frustration was the theme music from *Coronation Street* because it was distracting me from my very "important" meditation. But the music was just a sound. The disturbance was not in the sound but in my own mind. The frustration came from my views, opinions, and judgments about the sound. I was clinging to this moment being as I wanted it to be. I was creating the frustration, not my dear old mum. So the cause is my clinging to the moment being a certain way.

THIRD TRUTH: THERE IS AN END TO THIS FRUSTRATION

The Buddha's third truth is that there can be an end to mental and emotional suffering. We are not talking about physical pain here. The body will be painful, at least from time to time.

FOURTH TRUTH—HOW TO BRING THIS FRUSTRATION TO AN END

So there I am, sitting in meditation and going over the story in my mind about how unfair this is. I am sitting here being very spiritual indeed, and I have to put up with the theme music of *Coronation Street*. Couldn't my mum see how important my meditation is to the world?

So how to end this frustration? Well, the good news is that if the theme music was the source of my frustration, then there was probably not much I could do about it. If the external world is the source of our distress, then goodness helps us. We have no chance.

However, with a little awareness and honesty, I could see the source of the frustration: my own believed thoughts about how bad this is. What I needed to do in the situation was to identify the thoughts that I was getting hooked into.

So if I can identify these thoughts, such as "This shouldn't be happening; I don't like it," I can then let the thoughts go and come back to my breath. When I am not caught up with my thoughts about the situation, my frustration begins to ease. What I mean here is that we get caught in the storyline.

This is just one very simple example, of course, but the principle is always the same. My views, opinions, and judgments about the event create the emotional distress, not the event itself. In a sentence—don't disturb the sound.

I really like the four truths because they are practical and can be applied to every situation where we suffer. What I think is really incredible about the Buddha's teaching is that they don't start with a theory. His teaching doesn't begin with a proposition, with a theory. We can all argue about whether we have an eternal soul, or if we go to heaven or hell, or if we are reborn here into this world again. The truth is we don't really know. So his teachings don't start with a belief but with an experience we all share—that is, we suffer and so does everybody else. So instead of it evoking argument and conflict, it evokes sympathy and compassion. We are all in this together.

THE TWO DAGGERS

Let me explain by way of metaphor the Four Noble Truths. Let us say that something unfortunate has happened. It may be losing a job, getting ill, or losing a loved one. We all have unfortunate things happen to us.

We can see the unfortunate event as being stabbed by a dagger. It is painful. We are not trying to fool ourselves here. Nobody wants to get ill or lose a loved one; however, this is the metaphor of the two daggers. What happens when we are stabbed by that first dagger is to reach for a second one. Life stabs us with the first dagger, but we stab ourselves with the second. How do we do this? Well, just watch your mind here.

DOES A DOG HAVE MINDFULNESS?

I was once running a weekend retreat at our venue in Leicestershire in the United Kingdom. After a tea break, we were making our way back to the meditation space through the garden when we all came to a halt along the path.

I looked along the path and noticed our dog, Jaya, standing across the path in everybody's way. He was staring through the hedge at a cat or some other animal next door.

People often say to me on the courses and retreats that dogs and children are naturally mindful. But are they? Jaya was in the moment, but he had no awareness of other people and the context of the situation. He did not think to himself that he could move over to let the people past.

Mindfulness is not just about being in the present moment like our Jaya. It is knowing that our actions have consequences and that sometimes they can hurt other people or animals. Mindfulness is being aware of the situation we are in and the effect on other people. It is not a self-absorbed state. This state of mind is open and receptive to the world. It is a state of sensitivity to other people.

So when people tell me children and dogs are mindful, I disagree. I say they are present, but that is not enough. There is a world around us, other people around us, and we need to realize that very deeply.

MINDFUL WALKING AND THE BIRD FEEDER

I WANT TO give another example of the difference between mindfulness and concentration. Once a lovely Italian woman was training with me at our venue in Leicestershire in the United Kingdom.

She was leading a walking meditation and had set it up beautifully. She asked people to simply walk and to notice not only the movements of the body but also the movements of the mind. She also referred to the environment. We were in a delightful garden, so not only could we be aware of the environment, but also we needed to be mindful of where we were walking in case we tripped.

So Teresa set us going, and twelve of us set off around the garden, walking, of course, very mindfully. That was how it looked anyway. We know our body is always present but are our minds?

Anyway, Teresa was leading the way, and I noticed her looking down to the ground, looking very focused. Then I heard a tinging sound and a loud ouch! Teresa had hit her head on a birdfeeder hanging from the tree. It didn't hurt her, thankfully, and she saw the humor in it.

She then gathered us together and gave a great teaching from her own experience.

She said that she was concentrated but not mindful. She said she was focused on each and every step, the minute movements of each foot on the floor, but she was not aware of where she was or the world around her, and the fact that hanging from the tree was a birdfeeder.

This is classic. Of course, there is some need to concentrate, but the context that we are in must determine how much broader awareness we bring to the moment. Concentration can be practiced but always needs to be the servant to mindfulness.

It is no good being really concentrated on your loving-kindness meditation or any other meditation and then losing your temper when somebody knocks on your door.

There is no criticism at all of Teresa here, because no matter how long we have been practicing, we all miss these moments, and we all hit our head on the birdfeeder.

THE LAZY FISHERMAN

A sharp-suited businessman is walking to work along the seafront when he notices a shabbily dressed local fisherman taking a nap in his fishing boat. The businessman is disappointed with the fisherman's lazy attitude toward his work. He approaches the fisherman and asks him why he is lying around instead of catching fish. The fisherman explains that he went fishing in the morning, and the catch would be enough for the next few days. "But if you went out earlier, caught more fish, you could eventually buy a boat, then another, and eventually have a fleet of fishing boats. Then you could export the fish and become a really successful businessman like myself."

"Then what?" replies the fisherman.

"Well, you can enjoy life," says the businessman.

"But I am," replies the fisherman.

THERE IS A saying: "Busyness is really the height of laziness." Think about this.

RIDERS ON THE STORM

I LIKE THE Doors, the 1960s rock band. One of their classic tracks is "Riders on the Storm." It starts, "Riders on the storm. Into this house we're born. Into this world we're thrown. Like a dog without a bone. An actor out on loan. Riders on the storm." After many years of living in Buddhist communities and not listening to this rather raw and controversial music, it has been good to catch up with it again. When I first heard these lyrics in my late teens or twenties, I thought how true the words were.

I felt at the time that I had been thrown into this world and was ill equipped to deal with it. I never asked to be born; at least I don't recall doing so. But here I was in my late teens, and I was confused. I don't think I was alone in my confusion. I think this is the case with many of us, and for some, it may carry on well past teenage years. In fact, I think for most of us, it stays with us our whole life.

We are confused about life. We are like a dog without a bone. We don't know what to do with ourselves. When we are young, the adults around us are urging us to get to know what we want to do with our life. While the adults themselves have no real idea. They have just managed to bury this confusion under activity and many false ambitions. We come into this world with no tools so that we can work it all out. We find the world a threatening place, and so did members of the Doors who wrote "Riders on the Storm." There are many ways I am sure to begin to make sense of and live a good and wise life. Good religions can help, but many don't seem to. Good therapy can be a huge help to some people. Having a calling, a purpose where helping others is the aim of our life can be satisfying.

However, we all possess one tool that we can use to make sense of this life of ours, and that tool is awareness. Of course, it is no good having a tool if you don't know how to use it. Normally, we use our thinking mind to try to make sense of almost everything. As we have seen earlier, the thinking mind is a great tool, but it will never get us out of the shit we find ourselves in. In fact, the undisciplined thinking mind is responsible for getting us into this mess in the first place. We believe almost everything it tells us, which leaves us confused.

Most of us need a good meditation teacher to help us use awareness. We often need support and guidance. But there is one thing that all good teachers will tell you, and that is you need to sit quietly (call it meditation if you wish) and begin to see what is going on in your own mind. Most of us keep ourselves very busy so we don't have to see what is going on. Busyness is a strategy we use so we can avoid taking responsibility for our own unhappiness. When we sit quietly, we do the best single thing we can do for ourselves, and that is to face our own mind. If we know how to use awareness, then we can begin to see honestly just how attached we are to thinking and what we can do about it.

Awareness is not confused; when we identify with the contents of our mind—thoughts—we get confused. Thoughts come and go; one moment they are saying one thing, and the next moment something completely different. Chatter, chatter, chatter, all day long. No wonder we are ill at ease and distressed and confused. When we meditate or sit quietly, we begin to notice when we are lost in the confused thinking, and then we train our attention to return to awareness. We have to ride out the storm so that we can see what it is made from: our undisciplined mind.

We return it back to the breath, sounds, or a feeling of sadness. It doesn't really matter what we bring it back to. Slowly, over weeks, months, and years, we begin to trust not in our thinking mind but in something hidden deep within all of us. That something we can call intuitive awareness or our natural goodness, or some people would call it God. It doesn't matter what we call it, but to open to it we must. I may have made this sound easy—it isn't. We are all very attached to our story, our drama. But little by little, day after day, week after week, we begin to touch and listen to the wisdom within.

HOW TO BE TOTALLY UNHAPPY RIGHT NOW AND FOREVER

WHAT YOU PRACTICE is what you become very good at. That is why you practice. Well, many of us have been practicing being unhappy for a long time and are now very good at it indeed. If you wish to continue, here are a few pointers.

Compare yourself with others as much as possible.
Keep busy, and do not stop to rest and reflect on your life.
Keep complaining about everything and everybody.
Keep saying yes to everything people ask you to do.
Keep criticizing yourself and others.
Take everything said to you personally.
Take offence as much as possible.
Keep believing your thoughts.
Never ever trust your intuition.
Even better, deny there is such a thing.
Whatever you do, do not meditate.
Do your best to find happiness by pleasing other people.

Do what you think you should do.
Get in debt, as much as possible.
See yourself as a victim in this world.
Be with people who will never challenge you.
Be a perfectionist, always.
Procrastinate and never ever take risks.
Keep searching outside of yourself for that which will make you happy.
But most of all, never compliment other people, and do not give anything away.
And please add your own to this list, and keep doing them.

HOW TO BE (A LITTLE) HAPPIER RIGHT NOW AND FOREVER

A FEW YEARS ago, I gave a talk to a group of people at a local center. I called it "How to be a Little Happier Right Now and Forever." There were around eighty people, which was a lot more than usual. I sat for a few minutes then said I wanted to tell them how to be a bit happier right now and forever. I built it up a little with a little silence and pauses. Then I said, "Stop complaining." I then said thank you for coming, got up, and said good night. I was kidding, of course. I sat back down, and we meditated and chatted for the next hour or so. But in some ways, I meant it. If we stop moaning and complaining, we will immediately see a rise in our happiness levels.

Not great bliss or anything like that but significant difference. A woman on a course I led once said she realized that things didn't matter until she started moaning about them. This is so true. The weather doesn't matter until we moan about it. People criticizing us don't matter until we moan about it. The fact that we don't get what we want doesn't matter until we complain about it. I am not saying things don't need attending to, or if somebody does criticize us we should say something. But when we complain to ourselves, the conversations we have in our own heads lead us into misery.

Practice this—a day of noticing complaining: From the moment you put down this book, notice the urge to moan and complain. Notice the thoughts you want to spin with and let them go. Don't let yourself be dominated by these thoughts. Remember, they are like hooks. Unhook yourself and don't go with them. What you will notice is that you feel a lot more in control, a lot more present and that a certain amount of inner strength arises when we decide not to be a victim and spend our time moaning.

GIVING

I HAVE A habit of buying new bags. Yes, this is a confession. I see a nice-quality bag shop, and Upadana is there. I am hooked. Often when we are in Italy, which is where Gaynor, my wife, and I often go, I see a bag shop, and she will roll her eyes and mutter, "Oh no." I don't really deny myself if I want something. I am not a hoarder, though. When I buy a new bag, I give an old one away to a friend or a relative. I love doing this. One comes in, and one goes out. But I don't want anything for it. Sometimes I just like giving. It is a nice feeling. Perhaps that is what I get from it.

Somebody asked me a while ago why I give things away. My answer was why not. I mean it. Why not just give things away? I don't want to sell people my things. I just want to give them away. Our practice is giving too. Of course, we begin with ideas such as "I want to be happy," "I want to feel better," and "I want to be enlightened." These are OK to begin with, of course, but our practice must move beyond this.

We begin practice and hopefully we soon realize how self-obsessed we are. Our thoughts are all about us. If we were in the movies, we would all be Oscar winners. We are the star of the show that goes on in our head. As we progress with practice, we come to see more and more clearly that this way of living is unsatisfactory. A self-centered life is an unhappy life. If we have a good practice, we see again and again this self-obsession…thinking, thinking, thinking. A self-centered person has a head full of thoughts, and most of them are about him- or herself.

However, if we keep going through this difficult period, we begin to gradually give up this self-centered approach to life. We have been labeling our thoughts and being with the body sensations and now we are beginning to open up to the world around us. We then move onto the next stage of practice, which is to become much more concerned with how we affect other people. We come to see that our actions have consequences not just for ourselves but for others too.

We see that it is not just about how life treats us but about how we respond to life, to other people. We come to realize the world isn't there just to meet our needs and desires.

As practice matures, we begin to sense a big shift in our life. The shift from what I call the self-centered mode of living to a life-centered mode of living. We are no longer just interested in our own agenda for life. For what we can get out of it. We realize that we are here to surrender to life, to surrender our own ego-centered conditioning for the benefit of all. This is happiness. However, a word of caution: This is not achieved by setting up ideals of giving. This is not true giving. The giving I am talking about can only be done by seeing through the self-obsession we are all caught in.

KISA GOTAMI AND THE MUSTARD SEED

During Buddha's time, there lived a woman named Kisa Gotami. She had a young child, and one day the baby fell sick and died soon after. Kisa Gotami was so distraught that she refused to believe that her son was dead. She carried the body of her son around her village, asking if anyone could bring her son back to life.

She went to a number of teachers, and each in turn said he or she couldn't help her. However, one teacher said to her that the Buddha could help her. So off she went to see the Buddha. Kisa Gotami approached the Buddha and asked him if he could bring her baby back to life. "I can help you," said the Buddha, "but I need you to do something first."

"My Lord, I will do anything to bring my son back."

"I need you to go to that village over there and bring me a mustard seed, but it must be taken from a house

that has not known death. Bring this seed back to me, and I will help you."

Having great faith in the Buddha's promise, Kisa Gotami went from house to house, trying to find the mustard seed.

At the first house, a young woman offered to give her some mustard seeds. But when Kisa Gotami asked if she had ever lost a family member to death, the young women said her grandmother died a few months ago.

She moved on to the second house. A husband died a few years ago. The third house lost an uncle, and the fourth house lost a daughter. She kept moving from house to house, but the answer was all the same—every house had lost a family member to death.

Kisa Gotami finally came to realize that there is no one in the world who had never lost a family member to death. She now understood that death is inevitable and a natural part of life.

She took her grief to the Buddha and buried her son in the forest. She then returned to the Buddha and became his follower.

THIS IS ONE of my favorite stories from the Buddhist tradition. It brings up one or two questions. Why didn't the Buddha just tell her that everybody dies, that it is a natural part of life? That she needed to bury her son, go through the grieving process, and move on with her life? Firstly, it illustrates to me that when we are in the throes of strong emotion such as the death of a loved one, we don't see clearly. We can all deny reality when strong emotions take over. In Kisa's case, she could not come to terms with the death of her son.

Secondly, I think the Buddha wanted her to see from her own experience that she was not alone and that death is universal. Having the experience of knowing people die is different from being told people die. He wanted her to go through her grieving time, but she could only do that when she accepted the terrible situation.

Thirdly, seeing that other people had experienced the death of loved ones evoked sympathy and compassion in her. When we see that other people experience sadness and loss, it has the capacity to evoke what is best in us. I am sure there is a lot more to learn from the Kisa Gotami story.

THANKS

THANK YOU TO Charles and Steve—you know who you are. Charles and Steve kindly gave me sole use of their lovely Villa La Rota in Umbria, Italy, to finish this book. Thank you both for your kindness and generosity over the years.

A MINDFUL LIFE...JOIN THE COMMUNITY

IF YOU HAVE enjoyed this book and you would like to take things further and continue on your journey, then you can join our global community of practitioners living a mindful life. For example, if you would like to work toward establishing a meditation practice or you would like to deepen your existing one, then I have developed a program called A Mindful Life…continuing your journey.

A Mindful Life program is designed to support and guide you on your journey to living a mindful life. It involves teachings and meditations via video, podcasts, blogs, and live online "Ask Suryacitta" events. You can join us on our live online meditation evenings once a month via webinar, you can have one to one time with myself over skype or on a similar platform. The offer also includes signed copies of my books and access to all webinars which I run throughout the year, and more.

The monthly webinars I run which the program gives you access to are on a variety of themes such as "Help, I Can't Stop Thinking," "Stop Criticising, Start Living, Kick Chaos Out of Your Life for Good," and more. These webinars are interactive.

For more information go to **www.mindfulnesscic.co.uk/a-mindful-life**

RETREATS AND COURSES AROUND THE WORLD

If you would like to invite me to lead a retreat in your area then contact me on Suryacitta@gmail.com or, if would like to join me on a retreat or a course, then please go to the website **www.mindfulnesscic.co.uk**

FURTHER READING

Happiness and How It Happens—Finding Contentment through Mindfulness. The Happy Buddha—available from Amazon.

Mindfulness and Compassion—Embracing Life with Loving Kindness. The Happy Buddha—available from Amazon.

NOTES:

1 http://news.harvard.edu/gazette/story/2010/11/wandering-mind-not-a-happy-mind/

Printed in Great Britain
by Amazon